Dr. Maxine Lee-Fatt

GOD'S
LOVE
for All People

...Is Relentless!

WORKBOOK PRESS LLC
187 E Warm Springs Rd,
Suite B285, Las Vegas, NV 89119, USA
Website: https://workbookpress.com/
Hotline: 1-888-818-4856
Email: admin@workbookpress.com

Ordering Information:
Quantity sales. Special discounts are available on quantity purchases by corporations, associations, and others.
For details, contact the publisher at the address above.

Library of Congress Control Number:
ISBN-13:   978-1-958176-18-4 (Paperback Version)
                978-1-958176-19-1 (Digital Version

REV. DATE: 02/05/2022

God's Love for All
People . .

God's Love for
All People . . .

. . . Is Relentless

NO ONE IS LEFT OUT

Dr. Maxine Lee-Fatt

Dedication

This book is dedicated to my husband, Stan, and to my children — Wayne, Simone, Suzette — with love and many blessings.

CONTENTS

Acknowledgement

My sincere gratitude to all my teachers and professors who have encouraged me in my studies never to give up but to keep on striving, no matter the hardships or the difficulties ahead. To my parents, who have always inspired me to seek the path less traveled. I think of you always.

My thanks to my husband, Stan Lee-Fatt, and to my children — Wayne Lee-Fatt and his wife Paula Ramsay, Simone Lee-Fatt and Suzette Williams — who have unwaveringly supported all my efforts, however far-fetched they seemed. To my sisters Barbara Malchatsky and Karolle Kimmel, and my brothers-in-law Melvin Malchatsky and Jeffrey Kimmel, who have been supportive in all the avenues of endeavor that I have traversed.

To my dear friend Orville Green, who has been a tremendous help in the editorial process of this book. I am eternally grateful.

To my nieces Alexandra, Lucinda, Jeannette, her husband Oliver and daughter Lesley — you each hold a special place in my heart.

To my grandchildren and great-grandchildren - Quinn and his wife Georgia, Christian and his mother Olivia, Asia, Alexis, Sai, Aaron, Kalani, Ahviana, Quinn Jr., and Ahmir - may God love and protect you always. I love you all.

NO ONE IS LEFT OUT

This book attempts to reveal through selected Scripture verses — the diverse ways God demonstrates His love for each and everyone of His people.

Morning Prayer

Holy and Ever- Loving God, we awake this morning with aspirations of a blessed and peaceful day. Whatever unfolds over the course of this day, we place into Your most capable hands. We are forever grateful for your magnificent world — for the glow of the rising sun that wakes us at the dawn of a new day; for the chirping of birds looking for food as they fly by; for the vibrant color of an open rose in the garden outside – painted by Your very Fingers. We behold the variegated greenness of the huge magnolia tree, and the unique scent of a single flower; we revel in the unique smell of the earth — especially after a rainfall. We visualize the ocean with its cascading waves, thrusting against the shore, and again we marvel at the breathtaking brilliance of a spectacular world. Your creation is beyond comprehension — and we your people are forever grateful.

You have provided for our every need Oh Lord, although we are also aware that so many in our world struggle every day to put food on the table, and to provide adequately for their family. We ask you Lord that You will take care of their immediate needs — through the legitimate obligations of so many who are able, as well as through the goodness of others.

We thank you Lord for this precious life you have given us. We are all unique, irreplaceable, and purposefully knitted in our mother's womb.

We pray for our world this day, that those who are able — will show an act of kindness to someone else — even to a stranger. Help us to do this good deed — not just today, but

1

every day. If we can all do this, what an amazing world this would be!

This quiet time we spend with you each morning, Oh God, will serve to give us a sense of peace and serenity, a sense of quietude that we can carry with us throughout the day.

And finally, help us to make the right decisions this day, as we listen attentively to that small, still voice within us.

We love you Lord, and we praise your name, now and forever!

Amen and Amen!

Chapter 1 – NO ONE IS LEFT OUT

God saw everything that he had made, and indeed
it was very good. — **Genesis 1:31**

The entire creation that God has fashioned — "the Heavens and the Earth" -- is a creation that God continues to fashion, even today. God not only deemed His handiwork as good and fruitful and lasting, but one that was regarded as "very good" in His divine estimation. Creation itself is an ongoing process of beauty, to be cherished, to be protected and preserved for every succeeding generation, in order to give honor and glory to God. God's involvement in creation did not cease with a single act – creation is continuous, as God upholds our unique abilities and our cherished existence.

Let us together as human beings preserve this planet we inhabit by doing all we can to protect the natural resources we are privileged to enjoy. The result will be that every 'next' generation will enjoy the benefits, the inherent beauty and the resources of past generations. Each generation will add its own creative genius and unique fingerprint to our Earth's beauty, with the help of God's abiding guidance and with God's unending love.

In what ways are you attempting to preserve our planet for future generations?

3

"The Lord said to Moses (as The Lord speaks to all of his children), "I will do the very thing that you have asked; for you have found favor in my sight, and I know you by name." — **Exodus 33:17**

Yes, we are fortunate to worship a God who knows each one of us by name and calls us by name. He even knows the number of hair strands on our heads. Each and every one of us has a distinctive place in God's heart. So, when we pray to our heavenly Father, He listens to our request and He *always* answers our prayers. Sometimes, however, His answers may not be precisely as requested, but He answers us nonetheless.

Our duty is to trust God's word and to accept with love and humility the path He has laid out for us, His children, and follow Him faithfully. How do we come to know the path that God has chosen for us?

We listen very carefully to that still, small voice within us, and we follow God's lead wherever He takes us. In this way we can be assured of living a life that is permeated by the very presence, and singular goodness of God Almighty.

How carefully have you listened to that still, small voice within you? What comes to mind when you hear His voice?

> *"You shall be holy, for I the Lord your God, am holy."*
> — **Leviticus 19:2**

God is so in love with all His children and wants the very best for all peoples, that He desires everyone to acquire that special excellence, that goodness and that spirituality – that holiness – that He possesses, so that in all our ways, we may come to love and to imitate Him, the One who created us.

We imitate God by living our individual lives in keeping with His commandments, so that one day we may see Him, and be with Him for all eternity. God made us in His image and in His likeness, so let us then follow in God's footsteps and worship Him in goodness and in truth.

Let us strive for that holiness that can be ours by following God in word and in deed – as we ask God for the grace that we need to carry out His plan in our lives, in all that we do. Let us be vigilant in our pursuit to live a holy existence, one that is pleasing to God, a life that will draw us ever closer to the Living God.

What have you done recently that has made God smile?

"The Lord bless you and keep you; the Lord make his face shine upon you and be gracious to you; The Lord lift up his countenance upon you, and give you peace."
— **Numbers 6:24-26**

The Lord our God desires more than anything to shower upon His people His divine favors of blessings, grace, virtue, and peace. The light of His countenance is the font of eternal radiance that shines upon all of creation, as it provides the very sustenance of life-giving energy, fortitude, brilliance and well-being that we all need, to live a welladjusted and purposeful existence.

The Lord takes delight in His people, and He will bless us all our days, as we His children bless our God forever and ever, by worshiping Him by praising Him and by giving Him thanks for all the graces and benefits He has bestowed on all His children!

May the peace of Christ dwell within our hearts today, and always, as we serve Him with our whole hearts, by serving one another! May we be mindful of the many benefits we have received from a generous God and give praise and honor to His Majestic name forever and ever Amen!

What has brought profound peace into your life recently? What are the residual results of that peace?

"You are children of the Lord your God... you are a people holy to the Lord your God; it is you the Lord has chosen out of all the peoples on earth to be his people, his treasured possession." — **Deuteronomy 14:1**

We were uniquely chosen by God to live here on this earth. We were not randomly selected out of various possibilities, but we were hand-picked by God to live in this world, to laugh and to sing when

6

things are going the right way; to cry and to object when injustice is revealed; to sleep peacefully and to wake up refreshed each new day; to play and to be joyous when deemed appropriate; to eat modestly the delicious foods He has provided; and to treat each other as another 'self'.

We are God's chosen people, His most treasured prize, and His most valued possession. We are the pinnacle of God's creation.

Let us live then in our world as special, yet humble individuals, always cognizant of the fact that we are here on purpose, for a purpose.

Let us also be kind to one another, remembering that each of us has been uniquely chosen to share our world with others; we are to reach out to those most in need, to be respectful to those who cross our path, and to live joyously in the presence of our God.

To whom have you reached out recently, or lifted up out of their sorrow?

"As for me and my household, we will serve the Lord, and him we will obey." — **Joshua 24: 15, 24**

In the experiences of our lives, we come to recognize that the God who loves us so passionately, requires of us His children, total commitment, total dedication, and total love.

We demonstrate this obligation by serving the Lord our God with our whole heart, with our whole mind, with our whole soul; in effect, our entire being will serve our God, as we obey and give our hearts over to Him alone.

We will put God above all others, He will be the only God in our lives, He will be our God, and we will be His beloved people, destined to live with Him for all eternity.

This is how we serve God, and this is how we obey God — even in the ordinariness of everyday living.

Is our Heavenly Father the premier focus in your life?

> *"Where you go I will go; where you lodge I will lodge; your people shall be my people and your God my God."*
> — **Ruth 1:16**

The notion of going with, or walking with, another and to accompany him or her on life's journey, is the core message in this Scripture passage. It indicates a theology of accompaniment, togetherness, being with another on this our pilgrim's walk on earth. It signifies like mindedness, towards the people of God, for the people of God, and with the people of God. We were not placed on this earth to seek out a path for ourselves alone. God requires us to be in community with one another.

We are urged then to look out for one another as we traverse this land in which we all live. We are encouraged to share our resources with those most in need; we are inspired to take care of the orphans

8

and the widows, because when we take care of the 'least of these among us,' we are in fact taking care of Christ Himself.

Let us then seek out someone with whom we can travel on this pilgrim's journey of faith! Let us be prepared to give up something of ourselves, for the sake of another!

Whom will you accompany this day on their life's journey?

"Only fear the Lord, and serve him faithfully with all your heart; for consider what great things he has done for you." — **1 Samuel 12:24**

This passage speaks about "fear of the Lord". The fear mentioned here does not mean that we are to be afraid of God, or that we should be apprehensive about the idea of God. Instead, it means to reverence God, obey God, respect God, and to be in awe of the God who created us in His image and likeness. In this way we will actually serve Him earnestly and in truth.

And why should human beings be in awe of our heavenly Father? Because, first and foremost, God made us in the very likeness of Himself. Secondly, because of the magnificent gifts He has showered upon all His children for our benefit: gifts of grace, faith, holiness and truth. Thirdly, because of the intensity with which He protects and pursues His people. But most of all, because of the love He has for the entire world.

Therefore, we as human beings, respond with gratitude, with awe and with reverence for a mighty and awesome God, who has indeed done great things for all His people.

Can you name one great thing that God has done for you? Have you thanked Him?

> *"The Lord is my rock, my fortress, and my deliverer, my God, my rock in whom I take refuge, my shield and the horn of my salvation, my stronghold and my refuge, my savior… I call upon the Lord, who is worthy to be praised."* — **2 Samuel 22:2-4**

Our God is a defender of the weak, and a shelter for the weary. He is the Good Shepherd who protects His flock. There is no problem that is too complicated, and there is no issue that is too complex for God to handle.

Actually, God knows the extent of our concerns better than we ourselves know them; and what is even more astounding is that He is able to help us solve the most intricate and bothersome dilemma, if we only turn to Him for guidance.

God is indeed a solid rock on whom we can always depend, for He knows all things and He can do all things, Nothing is impossible with God, simply because He IS God – the God who cares deeply about the well-being of all His children!

So let us confidently cast our concerns into God's capable hands, and He will shield us from the ravages of an uncertain storm!

From what storm have you been protected?

"Blessed is the Lord who has given rest to his [children] according to all that he promised; not one word has failed of all his good promises, which he spoke through his [prophets]". — **1Kings 8:56**

The promise that the Lord our God has made to His people, throughout history, through the Scriptures, through the Church, through sacred tradition, in whatever context they were uttered, are grounded in divine truths; and those sacred and divine truths are dependable and they are trustworthy. God does not lie, nor can He utter a false word, because He is a God who is steeped in justice and might, and therefore no falsehood can emit from His divine lips.

Whenever God speaks, we as God's children can be assured that His spoken word is founded on wisdom. His word creates new vistas of understanding, and His word recreates and grants a fullness of spirit, in which all who reach out to Him will find goodness, purity and truth.

These truths that are ultimately from God are held as sacred teachings. They are to be listened to with a humble heart; and they are to be acted upon with wisdom and understanding, because our God is a gracious God, slow to anger, but He is of great kindness and compassion to all who call upon Him with a sincere, gentle and contrite heart.

When was the last time you reached out to God for comfort and solace? Remember we do not have to wait for a disaster to reach out to God. He delights in hearing from us - even when things are going well.

> *"Let the heavens be glad, and let the earth rejoice, and let them say among the nations, "The Lord is King!"* *"O give thanks to the Lord, for he is good; for his steadfast love endures forever."* — **1 Chronicles 16: 31, 34**

All in heaven and on earth cry out to God with joy, because we believe that God is our sovereign King. We believe that our God rules with a mighty outstretched hand to protect and guide the people of this earth, and the love that God has for all peoples is the kind of love that we humans should have for one another.

Remember how God guided the Israelites through the desert for forty years; how He fed them with manna when they were hungry; how He gave them water from a rock when they were thirsty; how He parted the Red Sea so that they could cross over on dry land to the promised land. This is the extent to which God will go for His people. This is an indication of what He will do for us today – He will see us through any difficulty and bring us safely to the other side.

We also believe that the love God has for all humanity stretches to the four corners of the world, and that love is everlasting, it is inclusive, it is constant and it is relentless. God so loved this world, that He was willing to give up His only Son, so that everyone who believes in Him will not perish, but will have everlasting life.

To what lengths will the Lord our God go for you and for me His beloved children? To the ends of the earth if necessary! He will go after the one lost sheep, so that His flock will be complete.

Have you wandered away from God's flock? Have you thought about returning?

"O Lord God of [all peoples], there is no God like you, in heaven or on earth, keeping covenant in steadfast love with your people, who walk before you with all their heart."… "God is good, and his steadfast love endures forever." — **2 Chronicles 6:14; 7:3**

Our God is a singular divine entity who is the creator, sovereign King, and omnipotent ruler over the heavens and the earth. God is love personified, a love that is steadfast, unchanging and unremitting. God showers His children with unflinching attention, particularly those who seek Him with their whole heart.

God is not only pure love, but God is entirely pure "good" — He is "good" personified. This love and this goodness that reveal who God is, is lavished upon all peoples throughout salvation history.

This steadfast love that God has for all His children has no comparison in this world – it is 'other worldly' – and yet, we humans are urged to emulate this love to the best of our natural ability.

We are encouraged to demonstrate this love to the people God has placed in our lives, and to extend this love to everyone we meet in our day-to-day experiences. We are urged not only to love those who love us, but in fact to love even those who have no love to give us in return.

In our human simplicity we may well ponder how God in His Divine purity could seek out and love a flawed sinner like me and like you? With God ALL things are possible. Even the most outlandish request we may dare to ask. So never be afraid to ask boldly and specifically - do all that you can to make it happen - and then leave the rest up to God.

Have you asked God for something specific recently?

Chapter 2 – GOD'S PROTECTION

[God] saw the distress of our ancestors and heard their cry. [God] performed signs and wonders against Pharaoh. [God] divided the sea before them, and so the [Israelites] passed through the sea on dry land. — **Nehemiah 9:9-11**

When we as God's children are in dire distress and we call upon Him to deliver us and save us from a potential disaster that is looming upon us, God hears our petitions and He answers our prayers in the way He sees fit.

Our response is to trust in Him and to accept the answer He provides, since it will be the very best solution to the situation at hand. Sometimes, however, we become stubborn and attempt to follow the dictates of our own choosing (like Pharaoh did), and the outcome can be disastrous.

Let us then be attuned to the ways of our God and follow the path He has carved out for each and every one of His children, so that we can live a joyous existence here on this earth, as we serve God, by serving each other, and caring for each other in the most loving and authentic way possible!

How have you served someone in need recently?

"As for me, I would seek God, and to God I would commit my cause. He does great things and unsearchable, marvelous things without number. He gives rain on the earth and sends waters to the fields; he sets on high those who are lowly, and those who mourn are lifted to safety."
– Job 5:8-11

We serve a God who takes care of all peoples and supplies the needs of the needy. God begins our day with the radiance of the sun to sustain our human bodies, and make our food crops flourish; and He ends our day with the glow of the moon, as He gives rest to our weary souls; He sends rain for our crops that we may enjoy the fruits of the land.

Those who are burdened and saddened by events in their lives are given hope for a brighter tomorrow.

This is the God we serve. This is the God in whom we trust. He will never leave us or abandon us to the uncertainties of this world. The important thing is to trust Him and turn over to Him those issues that we ourselves are unable to untangle, and God, in His time, will make all crooked paths straight.

He has promised us this, and we can be confident that He never breaks His word, because He is a giving and an approachable God, who is nearer to us than we can ever imagine!

Are you convinced that God will hold you upright when things around you seem to be collapsing?

> *"The Lord is my light and my salvation; whom shall I fear? The Lord is the stronghold of my life; of whom shall I be afraid?" ... "One thing I ask of the Lord, this I seek; to dwell in the house of the Lord all the days of my life, to behold the beauty of the Lord and contemplate his temple."* — **Psalm 27:1, 4**

If we believe in our heart that God is indeed our redeemer and savior, then we really have absolutely nothing to fear, because we understand that He is a mighty defender of His children, and will always come to our defense, whenever we call upon Him in faith.

When we come face-to-face with God in the Hereafter, there will be no more need for a light to guide our path because, having arrived at our final destination, we will be immersed in the glory of God's countenance and His magnificent light will be sufficient to illumine the splendor of His Kingdom, which will then include us, His children!

To dwell in the house of the Lord and worship Him in His Holy Temple – all the days of our lives – is the ultimate prayer in which we should invest. As we seek God above all things, we should pursue Him with every fiber of our being!

There is no greater calling, there is no loftier purpose that we His children could pursue!

Have you reached out recently and attempted to hold God's Hands?

"Be still and know that I am God! I am exalted among the nations. I am exalted in the earth." … "The Lord of hosts is with us; the God of Jacob is our refuge." — **Psalm 46:10-11**

Here we read about King David's reverence, devotion, and praise in the presence of our God. We are all assured that God is in fact Emanuel. God is not only our refuge and strength when the path before us seems desolate and unclear, but He is a God who is with us in times of abundant joy. The mighty Creator God is with us at all the seasons of our lives, since He dwells in the innermost recesses of the human heart.

We know that God will not force Himself into our hearts; it is left up to us to invite Him in, to reside with us, in the stillness of a heart that yearns and pines for the Living God.

Let us then, this day, throw wide open the doors of our heart, and invite God to come in and dine with us. Let us invite Him to live with us all the days of our lives; to be our refuge and strength, both in times of conflict and strife as well as in times of joyful abandon.

Have you felt God's presence in the extreme interior of your yearning heart?

"The Lord is my shepherd I shall not want. He makes me lie down in green pastures, he leads me beside still waters, he refreshes my soul." — **Psalm 23:1-2**

The Lord our God is the premier Shepherd of all His children. The shepherd protects His flock and He makes sure they are safe, that they are watered, and that they are fed. He sees to it that no harm will come upon them, and when we are tired and worn out from the pressures of the day, God provides a peaceful place for us to lay our head, so that we will be nourished and well rested for the events of the next day.

Then at the dawn of every new day, we rise up with renewed vigor and strength, in order to handle any and all eventualities that may come upon us. We open the gift of a new day with anticipation, with hope and with a new spirit of expectant joy.

We are assured that we are never alone, and that God is in our midst, waiting with bated breath for us to call upon Him, to acknowledge Him and to trust Him in all that we do. This is a God on whom we can depend, this is a God who protects and watches over all of His creation, particularly His human creation!

How have you been assured that God is in fact with you this day?

"Speak out for those who cannot speak, speak out for the rights of all of the destitute, speak out, judge righteously and defend the rights of the poor and needy." — **Proverbs 31:8-9**

As God's children on earth, we are given the distinct privilege of being God's eyes, God's hands, God's ears, God's feet and God's voice. We must therefore be very careful about what we look at, what we hold in our hands, what we hear, where we go and how we speak, since we see, hold, hear, walk and lend our voice on God's behalf, for all those who feel as if they have no voice in our society.

In this passage we are called to be particularly mindful to speak out and defend the rights of the poor and the marginalized, who may feel as if they do not have a voice or a say where they live.

As God's spokespersons, we have the awesome responsibility of securing justice for those who find themselves at the periphery of society. We, therefore, must be their voice for justice, and the voice for equality, for all peoples. We cannot be silent in the face of abuse of any kind, since God depends on us to care for each other, to be mindful of the plight of the other, and to act justly whenever we witness injustice of any kind.

How have you attempted to redress an injustice you have witnessed recently?

"For everything there is a season, and a time for everything under heaven:
A time to plant and a time to reap what is planted;
A time to break down and a time to build up;
A time to throw away and a time to gather;
A time to seek and a time to lose;
A time to keep silence and a time to speak." — **Ecclesiastes 3:1**

This passage reminds us that there are fixed time-frames concerning the events of our lives here on earth. None of us can do the same thing over and over again without changing the patterns of our routine. There is a time when we play because play is healthy, and there is another time when we must work because work is necessary. There is a time when we sleep, and there is another time when we are awake and active in the events of our lives.

There are times of our lives when we are engaged and focused on a particular situation, and then there are other times when we pull back from these situations. There is a time when we are young and energetic, and there is a time when we are older and filled with the wisdom of our years.

Let us be mindful to rejoice in all the seasons of our lives, and give thanks to God for all the changes that occur in the various seasons of our earthly existence.

How have you handled the various challenges that have occurred in your life? With open anticipation? or with resentment?

"Therefore the Lord waits to be gracious to you; therefore, he will rise up to show mercy to you. For the Lord is a God of justice; blessed are all those who wait for him." — **Isaiah 30:18**

The Prophet Isaiah speaks of God our Father as a creative potter who transforms clay (clay being His human creation) into instruments of beauty and value and worth. We are precious persons beloved by God, and we must be aware of who we are and how we contribute substantially to the world in which we live.

Let us then be confident of our worth and acknowledge a gracious and merciful God who sees us as we truly are — with all our defects – but loves us unconditionally; a God who loves us passionately, and who loves us purposefully.

Let us then, as God's children, learn to love our Creator-God, and love one another with our whole being. As God so loves us and cares for each and every one of His children, wherever they may live, in this wide, wonderful world of ours, so should we love and care for one another. This is the command God has for each and every one of us!

What are some of the ways you have demonstrated or shown your love for God?

"I have loved you with an everlasting love. Therefore, I have continued my faithfulness to you. You shall be my people and I will be your God." — **Jeremiah 31: 3, 30:22**

This unconditional love that God has for all peoples is again verbalized in the book of the prophet Jeremiah. Even when human beings turn their backs on God and follow their own devices, God is always at the ready to pull us back into His ever loving embrace when we return to Him in love, in truth and in faith.

22

God wants us to be truly His devoted and faithful followers, turning to face Him when things in our lives are going wonderfully, but especially when events in our lives are not going as we had planned, this is the time when we need Him the most.

The key to a solid and grounded relationship with our God is to trust Him in every area of our experiences, and listen when He speaks to us – through parents, through friends, through His Church, through our teachers – but most importantly when He speaks directly to our hearts. We are not only called to listen, but we are called upon to act on the prodding of our hearts and to decipher the right path we should follow, concerning the various events in our lives.

Has God "spoken" to you directly in that still small voice within? Or through someone else? Or in a dream?

"You have taken up my cause, O Lord, you have redeemed my life. You have seen the wrong done to me, O Lord; judge my cause." — **Lamentations 3: 58-59**

Sometimes in life we humans are judged unfairly and we are sometimes ostracized and rejected, perhaps through no fault of our own. We may feel abandoned by our friends, and deserted by our families, and we find ourselves alone in a cold and unfamiliar place.

But our God looks at our heart and He sees the truth of our circumstances; and He will come to our rescue and provide comfort and peace and restitution - if only we pour out our hearts to Him, and rely on Him to be our guide and our strength.

God will be an impartial judge, who knows our case fully. He will uphold the rights of a just cause, and defend us whenever and wherever injustice occurs. We have only to trust and obey Him in all that we do.

Even though we may never experience the resolution to an injustice that was done to us, we can be assured that in God's time He will handle it. In the meantime - Is there someone you need to forgive?

Chapter 3 – THE TALENTS WE POSSESS

"For he is the living God, enduring forever. His kingdom shall never be destroyed, and his domain has no end. He delivers and rescues, he works signs and wonders in heaven and on earth; for he has saved Daniel from the power of the lions." — **Daniel 6:26-27**

When the powers of this earth falsely conspire to denounce and cause harm to a godly person, God intervenes when we cry out to Him for help, and He listens to our petitions and He answers our prayers. Our God is just and merciful. He knows when His children are suffering unjustly and when we are being cruelly mistreated, and He always protects us from harm.

Daniel was thrown into the lion's den by pagan accusers, simply because he was praying to the one true God. But God saved him from harm and closed the lion's mouth, so that Daniel was not harmed. Miraculous events do happen in this life. We only have to believe and trust in the one true God.

Look out for these miracles! You will find them, because they happen every day, sometimes in tiny whispers, sometimes in loud refrain!

Praise be to God!

Now and forever!

What miracle have you witnessed recently? Miracles are all around us - all the time!

"It is I who answer and look after you. I am like an evergreen cypress; your faithfulness comes from me. Those who are wise understand these things; those who are discerning know them. For the ways of the Lord are right, and the upright walk in them." — **Hosea 14: 8-9**

We strive daily to be faithful in our relationship with God, simply because God has placed the seed of faith into our hearts and He has nursed it, watered it and fed it as we mature in holiness and in truth. After all, we are created in the image and likeness of God.

We are created out of love, and we are created in the love God has for each and every one of us. We are God-fearing people, and the allegiance we give back to God, is that original nucleus He had placed inside of us in the first place.

We belong to God and, according to St. Augustine, our heart remains restless, until it rests in God. We possess a God-vacuum within us, which only God can fill.

Let us then fill up that God-space within us. We do this by listening to His word, and by doing His will.

How has God filled up the 'God-space' within you? How do you respond to Him?

> *"He has told you O mortal, what is good; and what the*
> *Lord requires of you: But to do justice;*
> *And to love kindness;*
> *And to walk humbly with your God!"* — **Micah 6:8**

Micah was a minor prophet in the late Eight century BCE. And His message in the Eighth century still applies to us in the Twenty-first century. These three pivotal edicts are meaningful proclamations for all God's children to follow.

We are reminded that justice is an active word – it is a pursuit worth our time, our talent and our treasure, in which we must be engaged in the affairs of this world, and alleviate the burdens of the afflicted, in the best possible way, so that justice can prevail.

To love kindness is a humane responsibility: it means that we give without holding back; that we are considerate and we are generous. Kindness is an attribute that all humans should possess.

And lastly, we are encouraged to walk humbly with our God and Creator, knowing that God is Emanuel. He is a God who is not only "with us" but a God who watches over all peoples, at all times. Therefore, we walk humbly with our God, on our pilgrim's walk of faith!

Have you taken a walk with Jesus recently, in the cool of the evening?

"I will rejoice in the Lord; I will exult in the God of my salvation. God, the Lord, is my strength. He makes my feet like the feet of a deer, and makes me tread upon the heights." — **Habakkuk 3: 18-19**

When we immerse ourselves in God's divine presence, the burdens that would normally weigh us down are miraculously lifted, and we begin to soar on eagle's wings, because God is in fact our strength and our shield.

Besides, we each have guardian angels which God has sent to watch over us and protect us. We are doubly protected from the snares of entanglement, if we claim God as our rock and our defender.

So, let us soar like eagles, realizing that God will never allow us to fall. As long as we set our eyes on the face of our Father, and trust in His Son Jesus Christ, we will be guided along the way of everlasting truth.

[We may even tread upon water, as Peter did, if we remain focused on the face of our Lord and Savior!]

Have you been privileged to 'tread upon the heights'? How did it feel?

"At that time I will bring you home, at the time when I gather you; for I will make you renowned and praised among all the peoples of the earth, when I restore your fortunes before your eyes, says the Lord." — **Zephaniah 3:20**

When misfortune befalls us, and we become concerned, and afraid, we are urged at such times to cry out to God in our pain, and we must trust that God will correct any adversity we may experience. We believe that God will show us the path forward, so that we can once again rejoice in His presence.

At such times, we turn to God in faith — remembering that faith can move mountains — and our faith will lift us up; our faith will steady our feet and help us find a firm footing even on uneven ground, because we believe that God is definitely in control.

The key ingredient in a steadfast faith is a strong belief in a loving, caring, and compassionate God, who constantly watches over all His children.

Therefore, let us anchor our faith in our dependable God — like Zephaniah did — and trust Him in all our life experiences.

Even in a ferocious storm, are you firmly anchored to a dependable God?

"O Lord, you rule as King over all things, for the universe is in your power and there is no one who can oppose you when it is your will to save [your people], for you have made heaven and earth and every wonderful thing under heaven. You are Lord of all, and there is no one who can resist you, the Lord, because you know all things!" — **Esther 13:9**

God is all-seeing and all-knowing, and the Psalmist (David) reminds us that God Himself has knitted (created) us in our mother's womb. There is no place to which we can run and hide where God will not find us — however remote the place, however distant the land.

He is king over the entire world, and we are created on this earth to love, serve and worship Him, and to be with Him in the hereafter. God made us for Himself, and we never were, or never will be, some unknown entity, floundering about like a ship without a harbor.

We are God's people, the flock He guides. Let us respond in kind by loving God with our whole hearts and by loving our neighbor as we love ourselves. Only then will we be able to fully appreciate our awesome God and savior!

Only then can we begin to fathom the incomparable depth of God's love for all His children here on this earth!

In a disagreement with another, did you follow the promptings of your heart, as you considered your next move?

"For she (wisdom) is a breath of the power of God and a pure emanation of the glory of the Almighty; therefore, nothing [unclean] gains entrance into her. For she is a reflection of eternal light, a spotless mirror of the workings of God, and an image of his goodness." — **Wisdom of Solomon 7:25**

30

King Solomon, in his own writings concerning wisdom and understanding, has personified Wisdom itself as a woman who "is a breath of the power of God" and is also that which "emanates from the glory of God."

Wisdom, therefore, proceeds forth from God's divine being. Wisdom is a reflection of the divine light and she is also the representation of God's divine goodness. Whoever possesses wisdom is greatly blessed by God, is a child of God, and should be listened to with intense focus aiming at full understanding.

Let us, then, strive to acquire wisdom and understanding in our earthly endeavors, so that we too may better fathom the glorious splendor of God's kingdom, and sing of His mighty deeds!

We often hear about the Wisdom of Solomon. But this wisdom beckons to all of us from the depths of our soul. Have you listened to that voice clearly, what is the voice revealing?

"But the righteous live forever, and their reward is with the Lord; they will receive a glorious crown and a beautiful diadem from the hand of the Lord. For in everything, O Lord, you have exalted and glorified your people and have not neglected to help them, at all times and in all places."
— **Wisdom of Solomon 5:15; 19:22**

The guidance, protection, and favors that God showers on the righteous are evidenced throughout salvation history. God continually grants special benefits to those who follow His teachings, and obey His commandments.

Those who are filled with Wisdom are the virtuous ones who will be rewarded by God when He comes again; and they will be granted a special place in God's Kingdom, because they are the ones who have loved Him above all others and who have loved their neighbors as they love themselves.

These are the two greatest commandments, which all humans are urged to follow in all the circumstances of our lives: To love the Lord our God with all our heart, mind, soul and strength, and to love and care for each other, as we would love and care for our own selves!

What neighbor have you helped recently? - Remembering that a 'neighbor' can be the person across the street, or someone across the world from you.

"May your soul rejoice in God's mercy and may you never be ashamed to praise him. Do your work in good time, and in his own time, God will give you your reward." — **Sirach 51:29-30**

Each of us is uniquely placed on this earth for a particular function that no one else is capable of doing in the exact manner that we would accomplish it. Our task, therefore, is to determine what that special role might be, and do the work for which we were created, to the best of our ability. We should all strive to chase our truest calling, once we have determined exactly what that unique role may be.

If we are unsure or tentative about our creative ability, and how we may use it to build up God's kingdom, then we are encouraged to do some internal reflection as we carefully follow the burning desire that lodges at the very core of our being.

We ought to pray that God will direct our minds, our hearts, and our actions to that unique and singular purpose in our lives, to perform the unique task or tasks to which He has called us. In so doing, we will find that we will become fully satisfied with the work that we are called to do, for the greater glory of God, as we attempt to build up God's kingdom here on earth!

What is your unique talent with which you were blessed?

Chapter 4 – ASK AND YE SHALL RECEIVE

"You are the salt of the earth; but if salt has lost its taste, how can its saltiness be restored? It is no longer good for anything, but is thrown out and trampled underfoot. You are the light of the world. A city built on a hill cannot be hid. No one after lighting a lamp puts it under a bushel basket, but on a lampstand, and it gives light to the entire house." — Gospel of Matthew 5:13-15

When the children of God become truly aware of the generous gifts that God has so lavishly bestowed upon them, they are eager to share it with the rest of the world. They do not keep it hidden, but publicize it for the world to see. They "season" the earth as it were. As a result, the earth becomes a brighter and more lustrous place in which to live because we have uniquely "spiced up" the earth, and allowed our lamps to burn more brightly, wherever we go.

We dispel the darkness of doubt and separation as we share our gifts with those around us. We utilize our gifts for the greater glory of God, as we promote God's kingdom here on earth for the well-being of all creation.

Let us, therefore, allow our unique light to burn brightly in this life, for the benefit of our world!

What unique gift do you have that you are using to brighten our world?

> *"The Kingdom of heaven is like a merchant in search of fine pearls; on finding one pearl of great value, he went and sold all that he had and bought it."* — **The Gospel of Matthew, 13:45**

The Kingdom of Heaven is that sacred realm, that prized domain that we, as God's children, strive to inhabit in this life as well as in the life to come. It is a priceless avenue of endeavor that is worth all that we can give, in order to obtain a share of its glory.

We are urged to give up the false illusions of this earth and the inaccurate claims of many. Instead we should separate ourselves from those objects that eventually disappoint, and cling with all our being to the word of God in the Gospels, so that we too can claim a piece of God's divine abode.

Let us, therefore, not squander our time on this earth, but strive with all our might to secure a corner in this kingdom. Thus, we can behold God's glorious presence for all eternity, and live with God in the spiritual realm of perpetual Light, Peace and Love! Glorifying God and His heavenly kingdom as we enjoy God's everlasting splendor and majesty!

What in your possession would you sell in order to gain The Kingdom of God?

> *"Let the little children come to me, and do not stop them, for it is to such as these that the kingdom of heaven belongs."* — **Matthew 19:14**

God our Father reserves a special place in His heart for all His Children, since He emphasises that it is to these little children "that the kingdom of Heaven belongs". These children are destined for

God's heavenly glory, and for this very reason we, as adults, have a grave responsibility to cherish, protect, and guide them. But, above all, we are to love them unconditionally, as we direct their path towards their good — with God's ever-loving help.

Little children are placed into our care for a very short period of time. Consequently, we have a limited time-frame within which to mold and direct their thoughts, words and their actions -- so that they may grow into mature Christian adults, who will not only enjoy their earthly existence, but will subsequently live in God's heavenly kingdom for all eternity.

In what ways have you nurtured those around you, so that they will faithfully seek God and follow Him?

> *"They were astounded beyond measure saying "He (Jesus) has done everything well; he even makes the deaf to hear and the mute to speak."* — **The Gospel of Mark 7:37**

When Jesus lived on this earth — over two thousand years ago, He performed many miracles among the people who lived in the surrounding towns and villages He visited. They listened to His message of forgiveness, compassion, gratitude, obedience, and kindness to those most in need, and He showed concern and empathy for all peoples.

Most of all they witnessed the love he expressed for all humanity, even those considered to be His enemies. There was a distinct element of authenticity and trustworthiness in the way He spoke to the people He met, many of whom left everything behind, and followed Him when they were called.

It must be so with us living today. When we hear God's words proclaimed in Holy Scripture, we are encouraged to ponder in our hearts the message we hear and as a result, act upon them with conviction and purpose. In this way we, too, become followers of Jesus Christ, doing His will, and performing small as well as large miracles in our unique corners of the world.

How have you acted upon the Word of God - as found in the Scriptures, and how have you benefited from this knowledge?

> *Jesus teaching his disciples to pray: "Father, hallowed be your name, Your kingdom come. Your will be done on earth as it is in heaven, Give us each day our daily bread, and forgive us our sins, For we ourselves forgive everyone indebted to us. Lead us not into temptation, but deliver us from evil. Amen!"* — **Gospel of Luke 11:1-4**

When we pray we acknowledge God our Father as Holy and Righteous, and as the supreme creator of all that exists. We are aware that God's everlasting kingdom spans the heavens, the earth, and all that exists in our world. His kingdom is with, and for, all peoples — whether they believe it or not; whether they are aware of it or not; whether they accept it or not.

We ask God to provide not only the sustenance we need for our daily requirements, but we also ask for those things that will allow us to live a humane, respectful and dignified existence.

We beg for God's forgiveness each and every day, particularly for those wrongs we continue to do, both willingly and unwillingly, as we in turn must forgive those who offend us — both purposely as well as unwittingly.

We ask that God will keep all temptations away from our path; and even when tempted, we ask for the strength to walk away and not succumb to wrong-doing.

Lastly, we ask that God will deliver us from all evil, all danger and any harm that may be headed in our direction because, in many instances, God is the only protector and defender that we can count on, in times of hardship and distress.

How critical is The Our Father Prayer in your life? How faithfully do you follow the precepts therein?

Jesus speaks to us all: "Do not worry about your life, what you will eat, or about your body, what you will wear. For life is more than food, and the body more than clothing... For if God so clothes the grass of the field which is alive today and tomorrow is thrown into the oven, how much more will he clothe you — oh you of little faith." — **Gospel of Luke 12:22-23,28**

This message clearly suggests that God will in fact take care of all our urgent needs — whatever they may be. God already knows what our basic requirements are; they rest in His most capable hands, and we must trust that God will accomplish what He has promised. On our part, we are urged to place ourselves into God's protective care, and believe that He will complete the good works He has started within us, and bring them to a purposeful conclusion.

If God takes care of the very grass outside that has so very little value: how much more will He look after His human family, who are the very pinnacle of creation? How much more will He provide the essentials of ordinary living?

Our God knows exactly what we need, at the precise moment that we need it. Let us put our trust and faith in a dependable God, who listens to us, and who answers our prayers! God will never forsake us or abandon us to the winds of chance, or to the storms that hover around us.

What bothersome issue have you encountered in your life that steals the joy of living? Have you tried giving it up to God?

> *A Forgiving Father says to those of us who have strayed from his fold: "Quickly, bring out a robe – the best one – and put it on my [child]. Put a ring on the [child's] finger and sandals [for the child's] feet. And get a fatted calf and kill it, and let us eat and celebrate; for this [child] of mine was dead, but is alive again; was lost, but now is found."* — **The Gospel of Luke – 15:22**

At certain times in our lives, we may have turned our backs on God, in order to follow our own devices. Sometimes we may have strayed so far from God's embrace that we may feel completely lost and utterly forgotten, we may even feel as if there is no way back to God (as Judas Iscariot might have felt).

God, on the other hand, desperately wants us to make an about turn back to Him, with our whole being, and follow Him unflinchingly, deliberately and lovingly; so much so, that He waits with baited breath for our return to Him.

When we have come to our senses and we are sorry for offending Him, God is at the ready, as it were, to receive us back into the fold of His kingdom. God offers a sanctuary of love, relief, comfort, forgiveness and peace, as we rest securely in His arms. He is a welcoming God, who will leave the ninety-nine behind, so as to find and take care of the one lost sheep.

Remember that God is Love! So may we never be fearful of approaching Him when we find ourselves drifting in a direction that may be contrary to His teachings. We must never forget the love we may have experienced in the past, and so return to that familiar place of welcome and acknowledgment that awaits us, on our return to our Creator!

Have you wandered away from the protective arms of our Heavenly Father, and are you still afraid of returning to Him? Don't be. God is waiting for you with outstretched arms!

"For God so love the world that he gave his only begotten Son, so that everyone who believes in him may not perish, but may have eternal life."
— **The Gospel of John 3:16**

The above well-known and well-quoted Scripture passage clearly demonstrates the degree of love that God our Father has for ALL who believe in Him. Jesus said, "No one has greater love than this, but to lay down one's life for one's friends." (John 15:13). God Almighty loves the entire world — not some of the world, or part of the world, but the whole world, and not just some of the time, or part of the time — but He loves the whole world, ALL of the time!

God's love transcends time, space, geography, worlds, regions, nationalities, races, and communities. This indescribable and unfathomable love resulted in the divine becoming human in the person of Jesus Christ, who lived on the earth among ordinary human beings for thirty-three years.

Why would God send His only Son to live on this earth, and then to die on this earth - a Son who was both Human and Divine?

God sent His only Son into the world to rescue the human race from sin, and to show humanity how to live faithful lives; to show us how to treat each other; to show us how to forgive one-another; to show us how to be obedient to the Gospel teachings; to teach us how to pray; but most of all, to show us what eternal love looks like!

What in your experience would demonstrate what Eternal Love looks like? How does it feel?

> *"I give you a new commandment, that you love one another. Just as I have loved you, you also should love one another. By this everyone will know that you are my disciples, if you have love for one another."* — **The Gospel of John 13: 34-35**

41

The love God has for all humanity is not meant to be a one-sided affair. This love is meant to flow in two directions. God's love is extended to all human persons. Humans, on the other hand, should learn how to love God above all others, and to love each other as we love ourselves.

We are not meant to be selective with the love in our hearts. We are meant to share this love with those in our homes, with those in our community, and with those in our world.

How do we share our love with others?

We share our love by helping those most in need; by caring for the sick and the lonely; by sharing our God-given gifts — our time, our talents and our treasure — with others, particularly those who find themselves on the periphery of our society.

This is true discipleship, this is love in action, and this is how we as humans show our love here on earth!

What does your 'Love-Borometer' look like? Is it fully charged?

"Very truly I tell you, if you ask anything of the Father in my name, he will give it to you. Until now you have not asked for anything in my name. Ask and you shall receive, so that your joy may be complete." — **The Gospel of John, 16:23-24**

Jesus is telling us that when we pray, we must petition our heavenly Father for our needs — and we should do so in the name of His Son Jesus Christ. God clearly wants all His children to be joy-filled in this life. He wants us to be happy here on this earth.

Yet, we look around us, and this joy that we as humans should be feeling, seems to be eluding so many of us. Why is this so? Are we just not praying as we should? Are we not sincere in the way we pray? Are we not praying for the right things? Do we not believe that God will in fact answer our prayers?

Jesus tells us in Scripture that if we have faith as small as a mustard seed (the smallest of all seeds) we can say to any mountain, "Be lifted up and be transported to the sea," and this seemingly impossible event would happen, if it is said with utmost faith.

Let us then boldly go to our heavenly Father in prayer — and as we pray for our specific needs we do so in the name of His Son, Jesus Christ! And we must believe in our hearts that God hears us, and that he will answer our prayer. Jesus tells us in the Gospel: "Ask and you shall receive; seek and you shall find: knock and the door will be opened unto you."

This is a promise, and we believe in these words!

To your recollection — What prayers have been answered for you?

"I truly understand that God shows no partiality, but in every nation, anyone who fears him and does what is right, is acceptable to him." — **The Acts of the Apostles, 10:34-35**

43

God does not discriminate and He has no favorites among the faithful. All are equal in His sight among those who honor Him, those who are in awe of Him, those who worship Him, those who do justice, those who love kindness and those who walk humbly with Him! We are the people He shepherds; we are the flock He guides.

We, His people, strive daily in our unique experiences to be acceptable to Him, in all that we think, in all that we say, and in all that we do. We turn to Him in the ordinariness of our day-to-day encounters, as we are confident that God watches out for all of us, in the totality of our earthly existence! We cry out to God for deliverance when the storms of life seem to toss us about, when in our human way of thinking, there is no relief in sight.

It is at such times that we implicitly trust that God protects and defends the helpless and the forgotten – since He is the God of ALL that exists.

Therefore, He will not leave anyone defenseless; particularly those who are most in awe of God's magnificent kingship, as He relentlessly pursues all of us, in His incomprehensible and dynamic love for all humanity!

Can human beings strive to love one another even as God Loves us?

Chapter 5 – GOD IS LOVE

"For I am convinced that neither death, nor life, nor angels, nor rulers, nor things present, nor things to come, nor powers, nor height, nor depth, nor anything else in all creation will be able to separate us from the love of God in Christ Jesus our Lord."
— **Romans 8: 38-39**

What a powerful and reassuring statement concerning the extent and the magnitude to which God loves all humanity! We read in 1 John 4:8, that "God IS love." God is not *like* love, He is not *synonymous* with love, He does not *resemble* love, He does not *merely act like* He loves. Rather, He IS love!

45

God personifies love! He demonstrates how love acts, He showed how love sacrifices, He gave His all which is how love gives, His relationship with others illustrated how love interacts with others. God is love – yesterday, today, tomorrow, and forever. God will be forever LOVE! Therefore, no one, or no person on this earth can ever separate God from those who love God!

God's bond of love for the people He Shepherds is immediate, it is imminent, and it is everlasting!

Let us then draw closer and closer, day by day, to this one-of-a-kind, type of love; let us draw nearer to God, who is love! Because we know without a shadow of a doubt, that God is in love with *ALL* His children.

Can you feel God's love penetrating your heart? Stop a moment — and just feel it!

> *"Do you not know that your body is a temple of the Holy Spirit within you, which you have from God, and that you are not your own? For you were bought with a price; therefore, glorify God in your body."* — **The First Letter of St. Paul to the Corinthians, 6:19-20**

Each of us carries around within us, within our own bodies, God's Divine Holy Spirit, which was given to us by God. Think about that for a moment! What an awesome gift as well as a great responsibility that we as human beings share. It is that divine entity within us, the Spirit of God, who - if we take the time to listen very carefully – speaks to us, who directs, who instructs, who guides, and who propels us to act in accordance with God's divine purpose. We belong to God. We were purchased at a very high price.

Let us not squander the legacy of God's divine plan for our well-being.

St. Augustine affirmed that God made us for Himself, and one's heart is restless, until it rests in God.

Let us strive to serve God with every fiber of our being: To love Him above all others, as we cherish this temple of the Holy Spirit – our very bodies – to the glory and honor of God our creator and savior, so that when this earthly life is over, we may live with God in His Heavenly Kingdom for all eternity!

Right now, can you visualize Heaven and Eternity? As we spend our eternity with our Heavenly Father? What a glorious image!

"For in Jesus Christ every one of God's promises is a "yes". For this reason, it is through him that we say the "Amen", to the glory of God. But it is God who establishes us with you, in Christ, and has anointed us by putting his seal on us, and giving us his Spirit in our hearts."
"The grace of the Lord Jesus Christ, the love of God and the communion of the Holy Spirit be with you." — **The Second Letter of St. Paul to the Corinthians 1:20-22; 13:13**

When we pray, we do so 'to' the heavenly Father; it is 'through' Jesus Christ that we pray; and it is 'in' the Holy Spirit that we pray! And as the passage affirms, when we pray this way, God listens to our prayer, God hears our plea, and God responds to our requests.

When we close our prayer with the "Amen", we are acknowledging that God has heard us. The Amen in Hebrew means, 'certainly', or 'let it be so.' We conclude our prayer in the affirmative, with the understanding and the belief that our God, who is always with us and who knows us better than we know ourselves, has listened to our humble plea, and He will answer our prayer.

Sometimes, however, the answer that we receive may not be the outcome we desired or even asked for. But our faith is strong enough to accept God's response to us in the events of our lives, and we abide by the outcome that God reveals to us.

We are also convinced that God's Holy Spirit – the third person of the blessed trinity - dwells within us. This fact ought to give us pause, as we realize that the very Spirit of God our creator dwells within the very core of our human frame.

Let us therefore live confidently in the knowledge that the divine dwelling within us is an awesome reality!

Can you acknowledge the Holy Spirit living within you? And embrace Him or Her?

> *"The only thing that counts is faith working through love. For the whole law is summed up in a single commandment, "You shall love your neighbor as yourself." If we live by the Spirit, let us also be guided by the Spirit."* — **The Letter of St. Paul to the Galatians 5:6b, 14, 25.**

Faith working through love presupposes that we, as human beings, have fixed our hearts on the God of creation; and we strongly believe that God alone sustains, protects, guides and directs His children for

48

the ultimate good — to give praise and glory to God alone.

The love we carry in our hearts - which was placed there by God in the first place — exudes outward to the world around us. We become concerned, for the concerns of others; we cry when others hurt; we help in any way we can where and when we are needed; we go the extra mile for a just cause; we feed the hungry, clothe the naked, visit the sick; we give water to the thirsty.

This is what faith working through love looks like; this is how we love our neighbor as we love ourselves; this is how the Spirit of God guides us in all that we do, for the greater glory of God.

Have you witnessed your own faith working through the love in your heart? Write down the experience!

"For by grace we have been saved through faith and this is not your own doing, it is the gift of God - not the result of works, so that no one may boast. For we are what he has made us, created in Christ Jesus for good works, which God prepared beforehand, to be our way of life." — **The Letter of St. Paul to the Ephesians 2:8-10**

Our heavenly Father has seen fit to freely bestow upon the human race, His saving grace, so that those who believe in Him will have everlasting life. This grace cannot in any way be earned, bought, or otherwise acquired through the good works we do in our ordinary, day-to-day living.

Yes... it is absolutely necessary that we continue to do good works while we live on this earth — this is a worthwhile, rewarding and productive endeavor, and God applauds, encourages and acknowledges the good that we do, for the well-being of others. But it is God alone who bestows His divine grace on the human race. He alone decides where, when, how and to whom this grace is given.

Grace that is freely given to us requires a response from each and every one of God's children. It is not enough to hang on possessively to this grace — we are required to respond in a manner that is worthy of God's generous gift. We are expected to act in accordance with God's divine will, so that this grace will overflow our 'blessing' cup, as it drips into the saucer of our being!

In this way grace will bear fruit in the kingdom of God, not only for ourselves, but for those with whom we interact daily!

How have you experienced this "Blessing Cup" overflowing in the repository of your being?

"I am confident of this, that the one who has begun a good work among you, will bring it to completion by the day of Jesus Christ. I can do all things through him who strengthens me." — **The Letter of St. Paul to the Philippians, 1:6, 13.**

God who created all peoples, has gifted each and all of us with a particular talent that is unique to each person. No one else has the same skill set, the same point of view, the same talents, the same desires that I possess, or that you possess, bundled in the exact proportion as I do, or as you do.

We are all given separate and distinct abilities. And when we truly discover and appreciate the gifted individual that God has created, which happen to be "you" and "me", we will pursue that passion that lies within us, actively working-out our dreams to an astounding completion. Our God will surely bring our purposeful endeavors to a fruitful conclusion.

In fact, God will show us the way:

For His honor and for His glory!

For His purpose and for His design!

For His reign in His Divine Kingdom!

What unique gifts do you possess - and to what degree have you nurtured them?

"As God's chosen ones, holy and beloved, clothe yourself with compassion, kindness, humility, meekness and patience. Bear with one another and, if anyone has a complaint against another, forgive each other; just as the Lord has forgiven you, so you also must forgive. Above all, clothe yourself with love, which binds everything together in perfect harmony."
— **The Letter of St. Paul to the Colossians 3: 12-14**

Paul is reminding us, even today, that we too are God's children, and as such, we are urged to show compassion and patience, among other things, to all those persons we meet in our daily experiences. We are not in this world for our own purpose or design; but we are placed here on earth for each other, to extend a helping hand whenever a hand is needed.

We are not islands unto ourselves, alone and isolated from the rest of the world. We are to become engaged with the people we meet, to become a brother or a sister to the people around us, and we should become empathetic towards those issues that concern others. But most of all we are to love each other, even as God loves us unconditionally.

According to the well-known author Charles Chaput, "The love story between God and each one of us is unique and unrepeatable."

We know this because God sent His only Son into the world to give hope to the human race, to challenge us to challenge ourselves, to bind us together as one people-- just as the Father, Son, and the Holy Spirit are, indeed One God!

What does your love story with God look like? How have you sustained it?

"Now may our Lord Jesus Christ himself and God our Father, who loved us, and through grace, gave us eternal comfort and good hope, comfort your hearts and strengthen them in every good work and word." — **The Second Letter of St. Paul to the Thessalonians 2: 16-17**

52

When our hearts are heavy and disturbed about a particular problem, one that we are unable to solve to our own satisfaction, we turn to God our Father, through His Son — Jesus Christ — for comfort, solace, patience, but most of all for solutions.

God is at the ready to help us, if we invite Him into the situation and ask for His help. Sometimes His answers may not be easily discerned; so, after asking for help we must sit quietly with God and listen for His response, and we are urged to act upon the response we receive, realizing that if it came from God — then it is the most beneficial outcome we could have hoped for.

Lastly, we must always remember to thank God for all the answers we have received to prayers, and for the continued grace to discern that still small voice which speaks to us urgently, constantly and lovingly.

When was the last time that you told God that you love Him?

"For God did not give us a spirit of cowardice, but rather a spirit of power and of love and of self-discipline. Guard the good treasure entrusted to you, with the help of the Holy Spirit living in us." — **The Second Letter of St. Paul to Timothy, 1:7,14**

We are blessed and privileged children of God, endowed with His Divine Spirit living in the very depths of our being. As such, we should never be afraid to project and proclaim exactly who we are as God's people, and what we are about in this life. The talents which we have received so generously from God are to be developed, strengthened and proclaimed.

God has instilled in each and every one of us not only a unique gift, but also the where-with-all to promote this gift at every opportunity.

We have a distinct responsibility to protect this gift, to nurture it, to expand it, to advance it, and to share it with the rest of the world.

We ought not to hide from the world the 'treasure' that is within us. Instead, we must expose it to others as we give thanks to God for the benefits He has so lavishly showered upon us, for His glory, His power and His mighty reign upon this earth!

Let us always remember that at all times and in all places we should be eternally grateful for the graces that God continually pours out on His children, as we bear in mind that whatever we have in this life, whatever gifts we possess originally comes from a generous God, gifts that are not to be buried, but shouted from the rooftops!

Have you shared your unique gift from God with anyone? What was the outcome of the sharing?

"Let mutual love continue. Do not neglect to show hospitality to strangers, for by doing that, some have entertained angels without knowing it." — **The Letter to the Hebrews 13:1-2**

The unconditional love that God demonstrates to all people, is the same kind of love that we ought to extend to one another. God has given us an example to follow in His Son Jesus Christ, and we are encouraged to show this same kind of love to everyone we meet.

Love is not a commodity that we hang on to and keep locked up for ourselves. Love is demonstrated in action, an activity that must be shared with the people in our lives, as it comes alive by our thoughts, words and deeds. The love (hospitality) that we offer spontaneously to strangers could be that special gift that we might have unwittingly granted to God Himself, without even realizing exactly what we have done.

God sees our efforts and applauds our gestures of kindness and compassion -- even when, and especially when, they are extended to strangers, and particularly when our efforts demand a sacrifice on our part.

Ecclesiastes 11:1 states, "Cast your bread upon the waters; after a long time, you may find it again." This means that the good we do in this life — however unwittingly — however anonymously — can and will bear good fruit, if not immediately, then certainly in the days and years to come.

Which one of your gifts come to mind? How was it received?

"Listen my beloved [children]. Has not God chosen the poor of the world to be rich in faith and to be heirs of the kingdom that He has promised to those who love Him?"— **The Letter of St. James 2:5**

Whatever our position in this life, whether it is vast in worldly goods, or perhaps, we are poor in the eyes of the world, we are inspired to place our Creator God in the premier position of all that we do, all that we think, all that we feel and all that we experience.

But it is the poor that God has singled out for the rest of the world to give priority. The poor are with us to allow those with means to share in the excesses of their riches. The poor are to be taken seriously, they are to be taken care of, they are to be noticed, they are to be embraced, they are to be accepted and they are to be loved. We are in the world for one another, but the plight of the poor must tug at our heartstrings in such a way, that we cannot help but respond to their needs.

"There, but for the grace of God go I." We cannot turn our backs on those in need, since we can never be sure if and when we ourselves may be the ones in need of assistance, at some time in our lives.

We are obligated to help the poor as our means allow, for it is in helping the poor and the outcast that we may in fact be helping God

56

Himself, for the kingdom of God belongs to "the least of these among us."

How cognizant are you concerning the plight of the poor? How have you helped them?

> *"See what love the Father has given us that we should be called children of God; and that is what we are. The reason the world does not know us, is that it did not know him. Beloved we are God's children now; what we will be, has not yet been revealed. What we do know is this; when he is revealed, we will be like him, for we will see him as he is."* — **The First Letter of St. John 3:1**

God our Father wants all His children to realize that we are beloved, honored, and respected heirs of God's kingdom. We were created by love and in love, for God — to love God above all others and to love our neighbors as we love ourselves. We must never forget the basic premise of God's promise: that one day we will see God as He really is!

We are so loved by God, that whatever we ask in the name of His Son Jesus Christ, will be granted to us. Luke 11:9 states, "Ask and you shall receive; seek and you shall find; knock and the door will be opened to you." In our request, however, when we ask for something from God, we must always remember to add: "But may your mighty will be done!" What an amazing promise we have in the above quote. One day we will see God — and we will be with God for all eternity — as long as we love and obey Him.

Let us then do all that is humanly possible to live in a manner that is pleasing to God, to love God above all others and to love our neighbor as ourselves.

If each of us attempts to live by the golden rule — doing unto others as we would have them do unto us — what an amazing and spectacular world this would be!

We are ALL God's children, and He loves us beyond measure, beyond comprehension and beyond natural reason; for our God is a God of love and we, His earthly children, are eternally grateful, as we attempt to love God with every fiber of our being!

Can we as mere humans try to emulate that same love that God has for us? And spread it unsparingly to those we meet in this life?

Epilogue

We are placed in this life to love God above all others and to love our neighbor as we love ourselves. This is the most critical and the most important commandment that there is!

If we can accomplish these two things in the order stated, we will have done our part in this life.

None of us is an accident in the event of our birth. We are here on purpose for a purpose, to do a specific function. Let us not squander our precious time here on Earth.

Let us always and everywhere give God the honor and the glory due His name. Let us show reverence to the magnificence of Creation and acknowledge God as Creator and we, His people, as His most valued creation. Let us be mindful of those most in need among us and do whatever we can to help them. In this way we will be helping God Himself.

Prayer Petitions

1) We pray for peace and solidarity in our world –That God in His infinite goodness will protect us from: wars; viruses; unwanted disruptions; violence and hardships. That each of us will practice an act of kindness – everyday – for someone – especially a stranger.

2) _We pray for any Country suffering from the lack of the basic necessities of life, - food, water, and electricity - that world leaders and people of means will assist them in their struggle to live a fulfilled life.

3) We pray for elections everywhere, that they may be conducted with fairness and safety for all who choose to vote – and that elections may be accomplished without undue hardships or pressure.

4) We pray for all who have died– that they will be brought into the fold of God's welcoming and forgiving embrace, and may they enjoy a blissful and everlasting rest in their Heavenly Home.

5) We pray for the sick and the suffering – for those with chronic illnesses — may God give them strength and faith to manage whatever it is they are enduring.

6) We pray for all those affected with Covid-19 in this Country and around the world, that they will experience swift healing and strength to combat this disease.

7) We pray for all children in this Country and around the world. Lord, protect them from harm of any kind – including human trafficking. May laws be enacted to protect the most vulnerable among us. We pray also for those children with mental illnesses, that they may receive appropriate treatment for this devastating disorder.

8) We pray Lord that we may all draw closer and closer to You Oh God, and to love You as You deserve, and to treat others as we want to be treated. That the small sacrifices we may perform, may serve to strengthen our resolve to see Christ in the people around us. May our hearts and homes be open to your grace, that You so freely shower on each and every one of us, and may we in turn share our freely given grace, to the people with whom we interact on a daily basis.

9) We pray for an end to gun violence in this country and around the world, help us Oh God to seek a peaceful resolution to our conflicts, as we act like brothers and sisters to each other.

10) We pray for an end to Racial discrimination in our world, may God give us the hunger and the desire to live together in harmony and in peace.

11) We pray for ALL healthcare workers who serve the sick and the elderly, especially in the poorest Countries. Lord, may they be properly supported and appreciated by governments and local communities.

12) We pray for the recognition, and the appreciation of the dignity and respect that all human persons deserve– everywhere - that together, we may all acknowledge the

worthiness and the unique contribution we all contribute to our world.

Lord hear us – Lord Graciously hear us.

REFLECTIONS DURING THE TIME OF COVID AND ISOLATION

A time period of separation and aloneness, allows us an avenue of reflection and purposeful overview of our lives here on planet Earth.

In isolation, we find ourselves in an unfamiliar place, without family and friends around us. And we grieve the loss of the human touch, as we long for the time when familiar faces can be in proximity again.

So, alone with our thoughts, we may very well ask ourselves some profound questions, such as: what is my purpose here on Earth? What contribution can I offer to make this a better place in which to live? Am I living up to my full potential? What does God require from me?

Am I grateful for the opportunities that present themselves – either great or small, and to whom am I grateful? What path will I choose to follow – going forward?

Will I in this time of aloneness, create a space to advance – spiritually, relationally, creatively, gratefully, humanely? – in order to attain my God-given potential? Or will I march in place until I can again rush through the door and pick up where I left off – pre-Corona virus?

This is our time for meaningful reflection and contemplation about who we are, in what direction are we headed? and who can we bring along - on this new path going forward?

Make no mistake, we will all be changed – one way or another, as a result of social distancing and isolation in this time of Covid-19.

We may also ask ourselves, what are our Christian values– when things are going swimmingly well, or when we are hurting? These are challenging times for all of us. It is easy to say we believe, but when tested or challenged, how faithful are we? How deep are our commitments to Christ? – to take up our cross and follow Him – no matter what?

What is our Christian agenda? Our Christian agenda should be to Love God above all others, and to love and care for "the least among us."

In this sometimes-uncertain world, we all experience times of profound loss – the feeling in our core, a painful emptiness – and yet we also aspire and reach for a certain focused awareness of God, of ourselves, and of each other.

As we embrace our own cross – whatever that cross may look like, let us be generous to the hungry and eager to help the poor. We implore the Holy Spirit to allow us to always search for His or Her light and keep us in His or Her grace; to be with ALL of us – As we strive - To be One people – As God wants us to be.

We are urged also to reach out to our God, and, to say to Him three times – I love you Oh Lord; I love you Oh Lord; I love you Oh Lord! As we ask the Lord to come and live in us, so that we can become the salt of the earth, and the Light of the world. We ask the Lord to give us His Holy Spirit, the same Holy Spirit the early church received on Pentecost – and we receive Him in our hearts, in our homes, in our communities in our Country, and in our world!

In order to fully embrace God's Holy Spirit, we need to cultivate an intimate relationship with Him or Her – the same kind of relationship that Jesus had with His Father. When we lift up our eyes to heaven, we contemplate a God who is immanent, while at the same time, transcendent. Let us reflect on the God to whom we pray – the God in the Heavens, and the God who dwells in our hearts. Let us cling to the truth of God's word "your word oh Lord is a lamp for our feet and a guide for our path"

We are important to God, and He wants to be one, with us. Jesus wants us, His faithful followers, to be one with each other, as He is one with His heavenly Father. In this time of forced separation due to Covid-19, we may be physically separated from one another – but never are we separated from God. God's whole point of the incarnation was to show humanity that we are loved by God. And God wants to be connected spiritually with ALL of us. Because we are a gift from God – we should consider ourselves gifts to the people with whom we interact, as they are gifts to us as well.

Because of the times in which we now live, with Corona Virus always a possibility at our side, let us reflect on the distress so many are experiencing at this moment – some unable to go to church, some without a job, some unable to feed their families, some unable to visit relatives and friends in nursing homes, some unable to travel, and let us lift all of these distresses to our Lord. As

65

in Christ's suffering at His passion, and death – we are reminded that we are not alone – Christ is with us every step of the way. We are invited to tend the sheep and feed the flock the best way we can, (it could be with a smile to a stranger, it could be with a cup of water for the thirsty or it could be a kind word to the depressed) and we do these things with the love of God in our hearts. May we be Eucharist to one another as we feed, care for, love, serve, play and hold each other in prayer during this time of Covid-19 – and at all times.

As we lift our eyes in prayer to God, we bring the deep desires and the "stuff" of our lives, that fills our hearts and minds, before our loving God, as we let God's light shine on all of it. In the Gospels we read about Jesus at prayer and glimpse the intimacy and the depth of connection between Jesus and His Father. Jesus's prayer is about His disciples. This includes disciples mentioned in the bible, as well as you and me, who are called to be disciples as we follow Him.

Let us then raise our eyes to heaven and beg for a fuller share in the gifts of the Holy Spirit – gifts of wisdom, understanding, right judgement, courage, knowledge, reverence and the fear of the Lord, so that we too can enjoy the blessings promised to the faithful, and anticipate the joys we will receive in the hereafter in God's heavenly kingdom. And we also pray that ALL of us will come out at the end of this Pandemic-era, more humane, more generous, more compassionate to each other, loving God above all else and loving others as we love ourselves!

We ask all these things in Jesus's holy name!

Amen and Amen!!!

Dr. Maxine Lee-Fatt

A LOVE LETTER TO GOD

Dear God,

How can we mere human beings begin to love You, Oh God, with all our shortcomings, our flaws and our defections, as You so unflinchingly love each one of us Your children?

But in our limited capacity, in our inadequate mutterings, in our halting speech, we will attempt to express our love for You, Oh mighty and eternal God.

To just say - "I love you, Oh Lord - seems easy enough, but to feel the impact and the depth of those words, and to experience a kind of love that pours out of a human frame, directed to a Living, Awesome, Omnipotent and Everlasting God, is another level of aspiration. But we must start somewhere – even with our feeble words, and with our inadequate emotions – we reach up to the Heavens with love to an Omniscient, All-Powerful and Benevolent God.

And we say together,

I love You Oh Mighty God, with every fiber of my being; with every beat of my heart; with every glance that I take; with every sound that I make, with every step that I choose; and with every grasp of my hands. You are the lifeblood of my being, and without You, Oh God, I am but dust.

I depend on You for everything that I hold dear in this life and for everything that I experience as I go about my day. Without You Oh God I am nothing. If I must take another breath without You my God, let me not take it!

Your love sustains me; fulfills me; satisfies me and energizes me to accomplish whatever I do in this life. Your love for every human person cannot be measured – Your love is free-flowing; unending and replenishing as the air that I breathe. Yours is a love that never ends, and I crave this love in the totality of my being.

True love flows out in all directions. It is unselfish, it cannot be bought, it is grounded and at the same time it is air-bourn. The kind of love that You Oh God shed on all human beings is limitless, universal, unselfish and it will never diminish – even beyond the grave. This is the kind of love I yearn to give back to You Oh Omnipresent God.

Help me to attempt to capture and return to You, this very love that emanates from You, the same love you showed your followers, the love You expressed when you sojourned on this Earth. The same love You professed on the cross at Calvary – as you gave Your very life for the human race.

Help me to love You above all else, and to love my neighbor as I love myself – the two greatest commandments that all human beings are urged to feel and to show.

Help me to love as You LOVE, Oh Lord. You are the source of all that is good and all that is Holy, and I desire to imitate these traits – here on this Earth. Help me to show my love for you in the way I treat others, in the way I am mindful of the plight of the poor and in the ways in which I interact with those around me. Let me be a light in the darkness of those who are unable to see You; Let me be an instrument of your grace and your compassion in a suffering world. Let me be strong when the waves of this uncertain world surges in my direction.

You are my God, my life, my strength, my all!

I love You my Lord and my God – today, and ALL my tomorrows.

Amen and Amen!

My Prayer

Mighty and Amazing God, we, Your people give You thanks and praise for the many blessings we have received from You, and continue to receive, because of Your goodness, love, protection and care for all Your people. You have made us for Yourself in Your very image and likeness – to love You and to serve You – all the days of our lives, and for this reason we are restless and without an anchor or permanence, until we rest in Your protective embrace.

You have placed the sun and the moon, the stars and all the galaxies to reflect Your might and Your sovereign power. You, oh God, have given us the earth with everything that we ever need or desire; for our comfort and delight. There is none like You, oh God, in all the Creation.

May we, Your people, seek You untiringly; may we see Your handiwork in the striking colors of the rainbow; may we appreciate the artistic symmetry of a vibrant sunset; may we behold the dawning of a new day in the brilliance of a sunrise; may we delight in the laughter and contentment of a little child; may we revel in the deliberate gushing of a waterfall; may we inhale the majestic fragrance of a radiant rose painted by the fingertips of an amazing, incomprehensible and all-powerful God! Thank You, Lord, for loving Your human family with a love that stretches to the four corners of our world … and beyond!

The Our Father Prayer — Elaborated — by Dr. Maxine Lee-Fatt

The Our Father Prayer begins with the notion of grounding our relationship with the Father. The Disciples asked Jesus, "Lord, teach us how to pray" and the Our Father Prayer was born. St. Cyprian, of Carthage, a third century bishop commented," My dear friends, The Our Father prayer contains many great mysteries of our faith."

OUR FATHER

There is no question as to Who the Almighty God is, in relationship to every human soul who has walked the face of this planet earth we call home. He is our Abba, our Daddy, (or Dad). He is YHWH, He is Father to each and every one of us. So if we did not grow up with a father, did not know our earthly father, could not find our father, did not love or even like our own father, I have fantastic news for you — Our Father, who is also a God (imagine that) — loves, cherishes, protects, nourishes and watches over each and every one of us – God's beloved children — and He does this, not sometimes, not only when He feels like it — but each and every second, of each and every day.

WHO ART IN HEAVEN

We may have wondered from time to time where does God reside — where is God's home, dwelling, repair shop, location? Truth be told - God always resides everywhere, at the same time. God is omnipresent and resides in the very core of our being. God resides in our churches, in our workplaces, in our playgrounds, in our gardens, in the spectacular sunrise, in the breathtaking sunset, in the magnificent waterfalls, on the wings of a butterfly, in the laughter of a child, in the petal of a flower, in the air that we breathe. God is also present in the rooms of the sick, in the mortuary, on the sidewalk where so many homeless resides, and God exists in the homes of the wealthy. God is present in every galaxy that exists, after all, Our God created our world, and sustains our world. God exists where we are, as well as where we are not. God infiltrates every atom of the known, as well as the unknown world, and God exists in what is seen as well as what is unseen.

So then, if God exists in the core of our being, in our very hearts — can we then deduce an understanding, and the reality of acknowledging 'heaven' within a God-centered heart? I would say absolutely yes, we can! A heart that is clean, repentant and pure, a heart which welcomes God, and all things about God, could accommodate the motion that yes — an aspect of 'heaven' dwells within such a contrite and obedient heart.

HALLOWED BE YOUR NAME

God's Holy name, which is above all other names, is worthy of honor and praise. God's name — YHWH — is to be revered and glorified throughout human history. God's name is completely perfect, and completely whole. God's name is worthy of uncompromised devotion, a Name that should not be uttered flippantly or casually. We call upon God's name in reverence and with the deepest respect and awe. We are privileged as God's children and as Christians to call out to God, whenever and wherever we so desire. Knowing that God is never far away and is actually nearer to us than we can even fathom, and God waits with bated breath, to hear from each and every one of His children. God always listens to us when we call upon Him — and He does answer us — in His time and in His purposeful fashion. Psalm 48;10 states, "Your name, O God, like your praise, reaches to the ends of the earth." A name, that when spoken in imperative reflection, opens our hearts and our eyes to the needs of those around us, and the ways in which we can better serve them.

<u>YOUR KINGDOM COME</u>

The time of glory is fulfilled, God's domain is around us, God's kingdom has come upon humanity, with all perfection, in consummation, accomplishment and in completion — in truth, in beauty, in honesty, in fulfillment — and so much more! This is what God desires now, for all peoples – to live in that glorious kingdom — to embrace and infuse His very presence within every atom and cell of our being. Matthew 4: 17 states, "Repent, the Kingdom of heaven has come near." We can take ahold of this kingdom in our midst — and make it our own, with God's ever-outstretched arm. May we always recognize His kingdom, in the midst of a fractured world, and embrace its reality, with every breath that we take, and with every fiber of our being.

<u>YOUR WILL BE DONE</u>

God's will is clearly in Micah 6:8 'this is what our God requires of each and every one of us,' to seek justice (wherever it is lacking), to love kindness, (as we demonstrate benevolence to everyone who crosses our path), and to walk humbly with our God, (ALL the days of our lives) — The will of God is guaranteed to be the most resplendent reality that

74

exists for the human race. Sirach 32:14 states, "The one who seeks God's will, will accept His discipline as well." We ask that God's will be the standard by which we live and breathe and have our being. We implore that God's will, be the "pearl of great prize" that we yearn for — each day of our existence. God's will surpass all other wills, in substance, in function, and in action. If we as humans, attempt to follow God's will in all that we do — what a magnificent world this could be! Forsaking all other choices and clinging to God's purpose in all things. This could be Heaven on Earth! Forsaking all other "wills" as we cleave with all our strength — to God's steadfast desire for each one of us – God's beloved children.

ON EARTH AS IT IS IN HEAVEN

The God of Heaven and of this Earth, rules supremely. When we fully comprehend this basic principle of the order of our universe, and God's prerogative in it, we are better able to acknowledge and submit to the primacy of a God-endowed creation. God's will must be the preeminent Gospel to which all of us should cling. The human person was made in God's very image and in God's likeness — to serve and obey God — on this Earth — and to live with God for all eternity, and to serve others, as Jesus clearly demonstrated while he sojourned on this earth. This is the call we are to heed, this is our destiny, this is the "pearl" of great prize and price, for which we reach out. (Matt. 13:45-46). This is the crowning perfected glory for which we should be willing to give our lives — if we are so called to do.

GIVE US THIS DAY OUR DAILY BREAD (THE FIRST PETITION)

This request for bread here actually refers to those necessary items that we each require, each day of our lives. God provided manna for the Israelites in the desert as they escaped their oppressors. Jesus told His followers — "Do not worry about what you shall eat, or drink or wear. Our priority is to seek first the Kingdom of God - and all those earthly needs will be given to us as well, (Mt.6:25). We are urged to "ask, and we shall receive, seek and we shall find, knock and the door will be opened to us." (Mt. 7:7-11). We must ask God for the things we need in this life, and although He already knows exactly what we need - He hears our pleas, and He answers us — according to His divine wisdom and His purpose. We must learn to be specific with God — for whatever it is we are asking. We must not be vague with our request. Put a name and a number to our requests. Notice the plural "us" in the prayer. We not only pray for our own needs — but we include the needs of others as well. Friend and foe alike, the neighbor next door as well as the neighbor across the world. We are our brothers and sisters' keeper after all, and we were never made to be an island unto ourselves. We sink or we swim — together — as children of the Almighty God. Let us live our lives as if the life of our neighbor depended on how neighborly we act towards them.

FORGIVE US OUR TRESPASSES (SECOND PETITION)

No one attains perfection in this life, on this earth. We are all sinners, and we have all fallen short — noticeably short — of the glory of God. Proverbs 24: 16 states, "The righteous person stumble and fall (into sin) seven times per day." If this is the case, then we must perpetually ask God for forgiveness, several times during the day, through prayers, through almsgiving, through acts of charity, so that we can draw closer and closer to the Living God, the One who sustains us, watches over us, and who has even sent guardian angels to watch over us — every minute of every day. We thank the Lord that in so

76

many instances, God forgets certain wrongdoings we may have committed. (Isaiah 43:25) and the many times we may have turned away from Him, (Hebrews 10:17). We as God's children must seek forgiveness, not only for the sins we have committed, but we also ask forgiveness for the sins of our world.

AS WE FORGIVE THOSE WHO TRESPASS AGAINST US

If we ourselves are in need of constant forgiveness from God, for the many times we have offended Him, and turned away from Him, then the flip side of this equation is that we too must be ready and willing to forgive anyone who may have offended us — in word or in deed! We cannot in all good conscience ask for something that we ourselves are unwilling or unable to do for others, perhaps because of the perceived gravity of an offence. If this seems to be the case with us, then let us pray, "Lord, I ask you to forgive (name the person) who has done me this grave harm (name the harm) until I myself am willing and ready to do the same — with grace and with humility." Sirach 28:4 states, "If one has no mercy towards another, can he or she seek pardon for his or her own sin?" The answer is clearly no! If we want to be forgiven, then we too must be willing to forgive anyone who may have wronged us.

LEAD US NOT INTO TEMPTION (THIRD PETITION)

I have always had an issue or a question mark concerning this particular phrase or petition. Why on earth would God "lead us into temptation" (an exact Greek translation) to the extent that we have to ask for Him NOT to do this? This is not who God is! Would this not be better phrased or translated differently, if it expressly stated instead — "Help us to avoid temptation — at any cost; or "lead us away from temptation? When it entices us?

It is my understanding that Pope Francis has risked the wrath of the traditionalists and the originalists by approving a change to this particular phrase. Instead of saying "lead us not into temptation, it will now say, "Do not let us fall…." I fully approve of this new and improved wording. Thank the Lord!!

BUT DELIVER US FROM EVIL (FIFTH PETITION)

There are so many sinful traps into which we can be drawn. They exist in all areas of our lives. The notion of looking out only for ourselves, sometimes at the expense of others, or ignoring the beggar outside our front door, or not helping a neighbor in need, because we disagree with his or her politics – is not living a Godly existence. We may engage in habits that may initially appear as camouflaged "good". They are enticing and they may be bewitching. We are aware of what these actions are, as they tend to infiltrate the very soul of our being, one small action at a time. We may find it difficult to extricate ourselves from the hold this wrongdoing has on us. So we seek God's intervention to "deliver us" from this evil. We cannot rely on our own strength to overcome whatever torments us. God is at the ready to lift us out of any darkness we may encounter on this journey called life, and possibly even forget the wrong we may have done.

Ask and you shall receive!!!

FOR YOURS IS THE KINGDOM (THE DOXOLOGY)

"The Kingdom of Heaven has come near" (Matt. 14:7). And St. Mark adds "Repent and believe in the good news". This Kingdom belongs to God and His faithful followers, where all can enjoy the splendor of God in His prominence.

This Kingdom is everlasting, and God's dominion of this Kingdom endures throughout ALL generations. (Ps. 145:13). God's sovereignty of this domain cannot and will never be destroyed. (Daniel 7:14).

As a people of God, this is our destiny and our purpose, that God's everlasting Kingdom will be manifested in every heart! In the way we live our individual lives, by the way we look out for one another, by the way we treat "the least among us."

THE POWER AND THE GLORY

Yes, power and glory rightfully belong to God alone, and we His people are urged to demonstrate this fact in our prayers, and in our actions. We cannot attain our full potential unless God is steering our ship of life. We attribute this power and glory to God, not because He needs it, but because as God, we His children are urged to demonstrate our reverence and our awe to the God to whom we owe our very lives, recognizing that His dominion is everlasting, and His reign is eternal. Who else in heaven or on this earth can claim this distinction?

Let us always be cognizant of this reality and demonstrate this fact in our lives, by the way we love – by the way we love God, and by the way we love and treat our neighbor!

FOREVER AND EVER AMEN AND AMEN!!!

This prayer ends with solidifying our faith in the Kingship, power, and glory of God our Father. We owe God our very lives, as we are immersed in the very essence of His glory. This prayer summarizes the totality of reverence we attribute to a loving, caring, and compassionate God, after all, God instructed us to pray this unique and all-inclusive prayer.

This prayer, when prayed in a thoughtful and reverent manner, is heard, responded to and relished by a God who passionately loves each and every one of us — not sometimes, or when He feels like it — but perhaps when we least deserve it. This is the kind of God we serve. This is the Kind of God depicted in the parable of the Good Samaritan (Luke 10:25-37), and in the parable of The Prodigal son, also known as The Lost Son, Two Brothers, or the Loving Father (Luke 15:11-32). Theodore Parker, the 19th century Unitarian minister once said, "I do not pretend to understand the moral universe. The arc is a long one, my eye reaches but little ways."

My own eyes and heart may not have captured all the relevant and pertinent issues of this magnificent and all-inclusive "Our Father Prayer", but in my humble and insignificant manner, I hope I may have opened some new doors to this powerful prayer, for even one person.

May God in His infinite goodness protect and guide us all the days of our lives. And when this sojourn on earth is over, may we live with Him for all eternity!!

Amen and Amen!!!

EVENING PRAYER

Holy and Dependable God, we have come to the end of a fruitful day, and you have blessed us with your presence and with your guidance this day. We thank You Oh God that You have brought us safely home from the various activities of our day, and that You have provided for our daily needs, as You deemed appropriate.

We humbly ask your blessings Oh Lord on our family and on our friends. We pray for all those who are sick, (name them) as we humbly ask for their speedy recovery. We pray for those who live alone — because they have lost a loved one. Comfort them in their sorrow and in their loneliness.

If we have failed you unwittingly in any way this day Lord, we humbly ask for Your forgiveness, if we have spoken a harsh word, or ignored the need of another, we ask that You help us to do better tomorrow.

We pray for our world Oh God, that peace will triumph over war, that kindness will reign in the hearts of everyone, everywhere! That wealthier nations will choose to help their neighbors who are less fortunate and who are in desperate need of the basic necessities of this life.

May we choose peace and reconciliation in these United States — may we truly be united in the way we treat each other, regardless of race, color or creed.

As this day draws to a close, we pray for a restful night, to lay peacefully in your protective Arms.

May those who choose to do harm to others, experience a change of heart — and do the good that hopefully lies somewhere in their souls.

We rest All Things Oh God in Your most extraordinary Hands — this night and always.

Graciously hear our humble prayer this night — our Lord and our God!

Amen and Amen!

Ingram Content Group UK Ltd.
Milton Keynes UK
UKHW020022100323
418330UK00009B/533

9 781958 176184